S CLUB 7 '7'

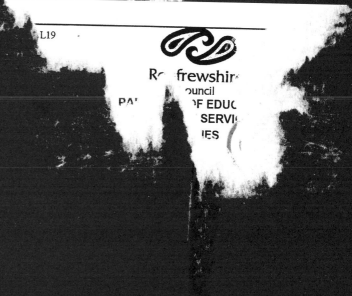

Exclusive distributors:
Music Sales Limited
8/9 Frith Street,
London W1D 3JB, England.
Music Sales Pty Limited
120 Rothschild Avenue
Rosebery, NSW 2018,
Australia.

Order No.AM968583
ISBN 0-7119-8650-9
This book © Copyright 2000 by Wise Publications

Music Sales' complete catalogue describes thousands of titles and is available in full colour sections by subject, direct from Music Sales Limited. Please state your areas of interest and send a cheque/postal order for £1.50 for postage to: Music Sales Limited, Newmarket Road, Bury St. Edmunds, Suffolk IP33 3YB.

www.musicsales.com

S CLUB 7

'7'

Reach

Words and Music by
Cathy Dennis and Andrew Todd

1.(F) When the world leaves you feel-ing blue you— can
2.(M) There's a place wait-ing just for you. It's— a

count on me.
spe-cial place

I will be there for— you.
where— your dreams all come— true.

Natural

Words and Music by
Norma Ray, Jean Fredenucci, Cathy Dennis,
and Andrew Todd

Adapted from the song 'Tous Les Maux D'Amour' (Words & Music by Norma Ray & Jean Fredenucci). Contains an extract of 'Pavane' by Gabriel Fauré.
© 2000 M6 Interactions/BRJ Music/Jean Fredenucci/EMI Music Publishing Ltd, London WC2H 0QY and BMG Music Publishing Ltd, Bedford House,
69-79 Fulham High Street, London SW6

Turn off the light, lay your head next to mine,— take it slow-ly, a step at a time.—

Come on get close, get clos-er to me,— it's all so na-tu-ral, it's all so ea-sy to see.— Ba-by, lov-ing

you— comes ea-si-ly to me, it's what I'm liv-ing for,— it's all in the che-mis-try.— Ba-by, lov-ing

Repeat ad lib. to fade

you— is how it's meant to be,— it's some-thing that is oh so na-tu-ral to me. Ba-by lov-ing

I'll Keep Waiting

Words and Music by
Cathy Dennis and Simon Ellis

Spoken: Been a long time girl   but I keep on waiting.

I'll keep wait-ing 'til that day when you come back on___ home to me.

Life's too short___ to live with-out you, where you are is___ where I wan-na

Bring The House Down

Words and Music by
Andy Watkins, Paul Wilson and Tracy Ackerman

Best Friend

Words and Music by
Timothy Laws, Stephen Emmanuel
and Bradley McIntosh

All In Love Is Fair

Words and Music by
Cathy Dennis and Simon Ellis

Love Train

Words and Music by
Cathy Dennis and Andrew Todd

Cross My Heart

Words and Music by
Andy Watkins, Paul Wilson
and Tracy Ackerman

Repeat ad lib. to fade

The Colour Of Blue

Words and Music by
Lars Aass and Bottolf Lødemel

I'll Be There

Words and Music by
Cathy Dennis and Danny D

I'll be there for— you.—

Do, do, do, do, do, do, do,

Stand By You

Words and Music by
Remee and Kristian Holger

Spiritual Love

Words and Music by
Peter Akinrinlola and Rodney Green

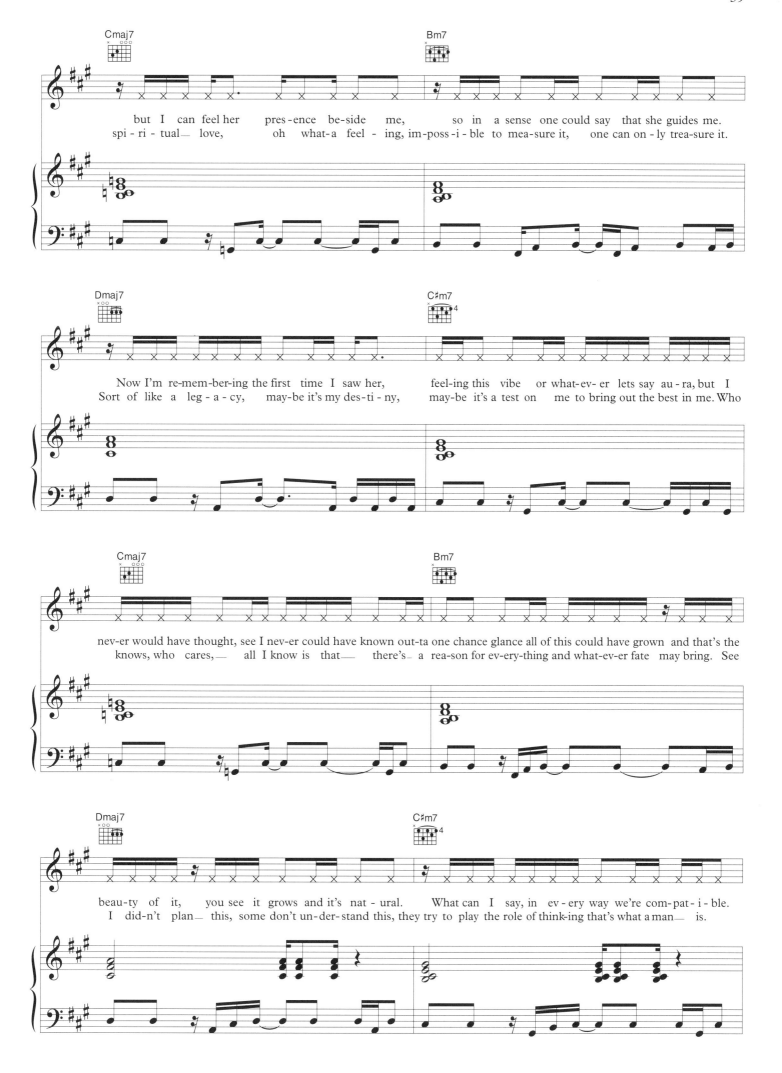

Printed and bound in Great Britain 4/01